The Fish King

The Fish King

Illustrated by Bradley Clemmons and Julia Witwer

DHARMA  PUBLISHING

First published 1987

Second edition 2009, augmented with guidance
for parents and teachers

Printed on acid-free paper
Printed in the United States of America by Dharma Press
35788 Hauser Bridge Road, Cazadero, California 95421

9   8   7   6   5   4   3   2   1

Library of Congress Cataloging-in-Publication Data

Mi-pham-rgya-mtsho, 'Jam-mgon 'Ju, 1846-1912
The Fish King's Power of Truth

(Jataka Tales Series)
Summary: When the water level in his lake becomes dangerously low, the
Fisk King prays for rain to save himself and his fellow fish.

Jataka stories, English. [1. Jataka stories]
I. Clemmons, Bradley and Witwer, Julia, ill. II. Series
BQ1462.E5 M35   1986   294.3'823   86-24159

ISBN 978-0-89800-491-5

Dedicated to children everywhere

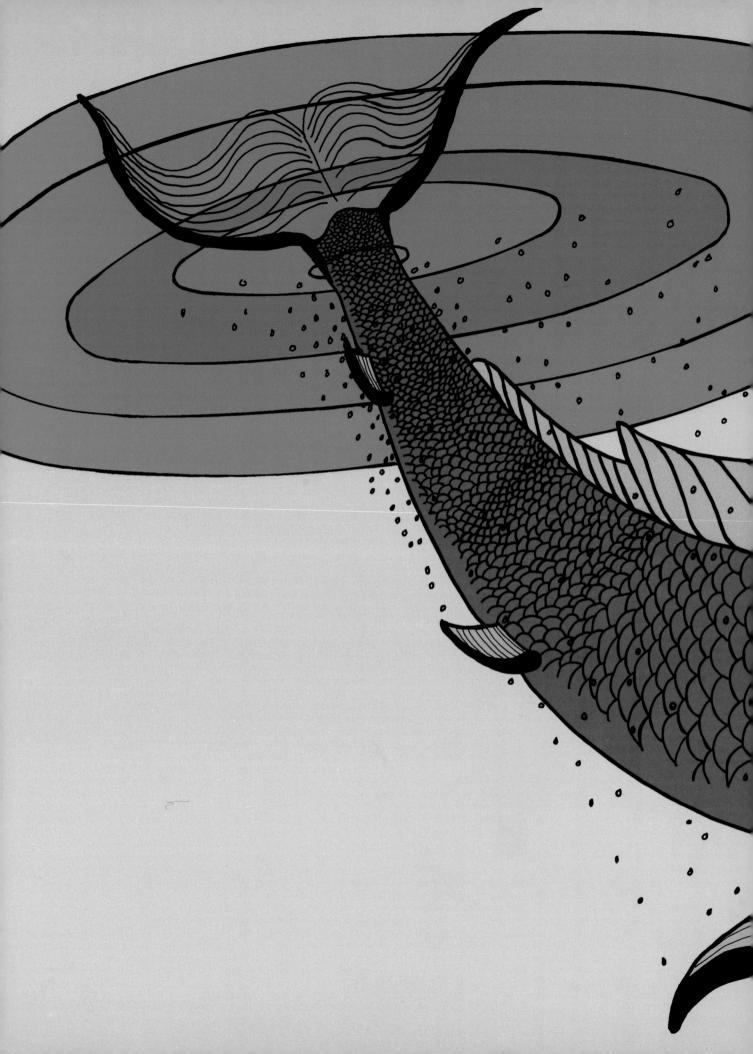

Once upon a time in the far-off land of India there lived a great fish, a majestic king of fishes.

The Fish King lived in a small lake dotted with red and white lotuses and surrounded by mountain peaks and meadows. In the lake, fish, tortoises and other animals of all sizes, shapes, and colors lived together happily.

The Fish King loved the creatures in the little lake as if they were his children. He helped them whenever he could and taught them never to harm one another. Under his guidance they prospered and grew plump and healthy.

One year the winter rains did not come, and
by springtime the lake began to dry up.
As summer drew near, the days grew hot,
and a dry wind blew over the lake.
Each day the lake became
smaller and smaller.

The fish and other creatures in the lake were
frightened and distressed. Soon they were
so crowded that they had to bury
themselves in the mud.

Watching them the Fish King thought:
"My poor friends will soon be dying."

When the lake had shrunk to the size of a small pond, hawks, crows and other fish-eating birds began to gather around it, knowing that soon they could catch all the fish they wanted. The Fish King thought, "Our home grows smaller each day. And how can we ever escape these birds? There seems to be no way out. What can be done?"

At that moment the love in his heart showed him a way to save his friends. The mighty fish swam up from the mud of the lake bottom. Then, he lifted his head out of the water. Looking up to the realm of Shakra, king of the sky-dwelling beings, he said: "No matter how desperate we are for food and safety, we will never harm each other. As this is the truth, may the ruler of the skies bring forth rain to fill up the lake, and cause thunder and lightning to chase away the birds."

Hearing the Fish King's words and knowing them to be true, the gods and the forces of nature mustered their power together. They shaped huge clouds and made them fat with rain. They decorated the clouds with lightning and filled the air with the music of thunder. Soon raindrops were falling like strings of pearls. Water flowed on the ground and poured into the lake in torrents. Alarmed, the crows and hawks and other fish-eating birds flew off.

As the lake filled up, the Fish King's heart was filled with joy. But the rain did not stop; soon the fields would be flooded and the land animals driven from their homes. Once again lifting himself out of the water, the Fish King cried out, "O, clouds with your thunder and lightning, you have rained long enough. We have all the water we need. We are grateful for your generosity, but please stop now!" At once the rain stopped. The clouds became thinner, and the sun shone down softly, warming the lake.

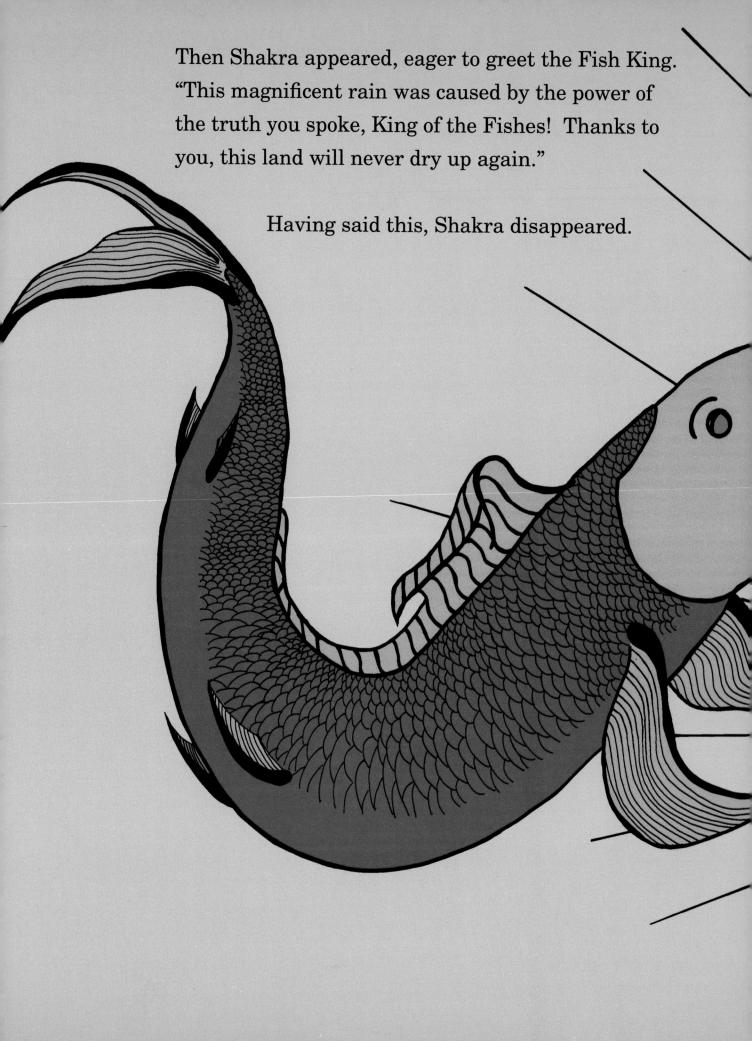

Then Shakra appeared, eager to greet the Fish King. "This magnificent rain was caused by the power of the truth you spoke, King of the Fishes! Thanks to you, this land will never dry up again."

Having said this, Shakra disappeared.

Ever afterward, the rains came on time each year, and the lake and the meadows around it became more bountiful. For many years thereafter, the Fish King and his friends lived happily in their fragrant, lotus-filled lake.

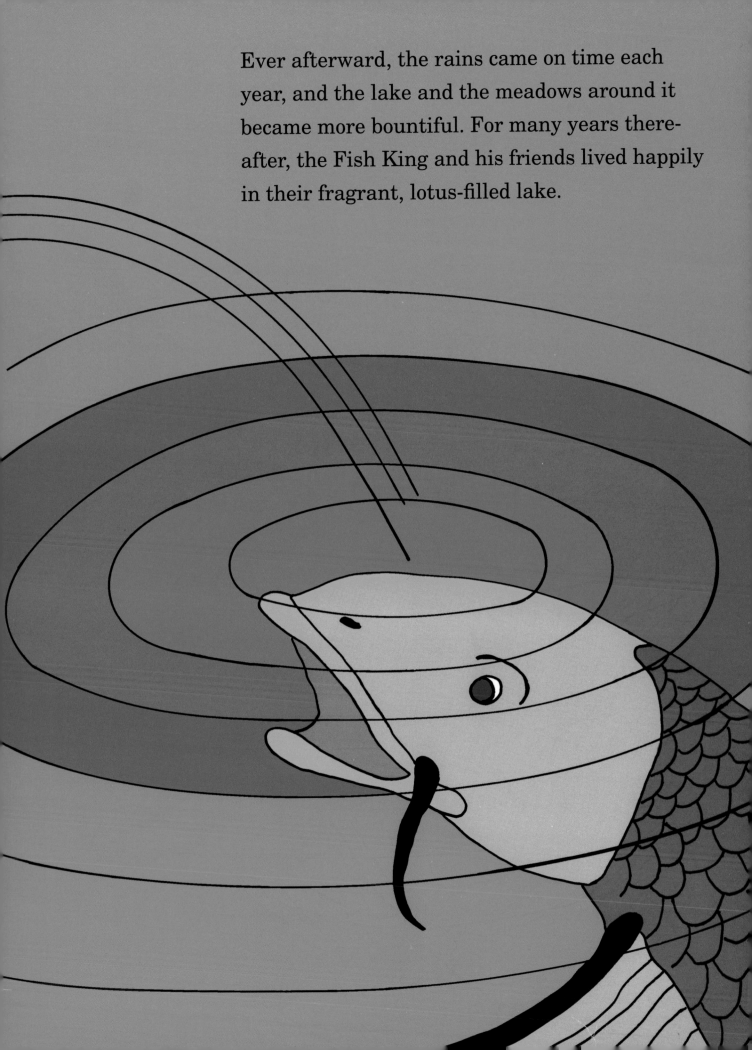

My Page

Colored by_____

PARENTS' AND TEACHERS' CORNER

The Jataka Tales nurture in readers young and old an appreciation for values shared by all the world's great traditions. Read aloud, performed and studied for centuries, they communicate universal values such as kindness, forgiveness, compassion, humility, courage, honesty and patience. You can bring these stories alive through the suggestions on these pages. Actively engaging with the stories creates a bridge to the children in your life and opens a dialogue about what brings joy, stability and caring.

The Fish King

The king of the fishes is devoted to the happiness and well-being of all the creatures in the lotus-filled lake. When one year the spring rains do not come, the lake begins to dry up. Knowing his friends are in great danger, the Fish King draws upon the power of his past virtuous actions. Based on this truth, he implores the god Shakra to restore the lake and save all the beings in it. His virtue is so powerful that Shakra is compelled to obey.

Key values
Goodness
Wise use of resources
Non-violence

Bringing the story to life

Engage the children by asking: "This tale is about a Fish King whose subjects are threatened when the lake dries up. What might happen next?" Ask what they think will happen next each time you turn the page.

You can draw children into the values of the story by asking questions that both help them understand the plot and let them think about the implications of their own actions. For example:

- Why does the lake dry up? What will happen if it does?
- Why do the birds flock around the lake?
- For whom does the Fish King feel responsible?
- Why does Shakra respond to the Fish King's request?
- If you were the Fish King, would you have thought to stop the rain from falling?
- How are good deeds powerful?

Discussion topics and questions can be modified depending on the child's age.

Teaching values through play

Follow up on the storytelling with creative activities that explore the characters and values and appeal to the five senses.

- Have the children color in or draw a scene or character that intrigues them. Then invite them to talk about what it means to them, exploring key values.
- Construct and decorate masks for each character: Then have the children act out different parts of the story, playing the Fish King, Shakra, the fish-eating birds.
- Bring up a difficult or challenging situation in the child's current life; using the drawings and masks, ask him or her questions such as: "What would the Fish King say?"
- Have the children retell you the story in their own words. Ask them to give the story a different ending.

Active reading

Before children can read, they enjoy story telling and love growing familiar with the characters and drawings. You can just show them the pictures and tell the story in your own words.

- Children like to hear the same story over and over, with characteristic voices for each animal. When you vary the voice and rhythm of a telling, it comes alive for listener and teller.
- Integrate the wisdom of the story into everyday life. When there is an opportunity for honesty and asking for help, remind the children of the strength of good actions.
- Carry a book whenever you leave the house in case there is some extra time for reading.
- Talk about the story with your child while you are engaged in daily activities like washing the dishes or driving to school. "
- Display the key values on the refrigerator or a bulletin board – at child's eye level.

Names and places

India: A country in Asia; the source of many spiritual traditions and the background of most of the Jataka tales. The Jatakas clarify the workings of karma and illustrate the relationship between actions and results.

Monsoon: The monsoon of the Indian continent is a seasonal wind that brings heavy downpour of rain from June through September. The land lives on the stored-up water until June, when the cycle starts over.

Shakra: Also known as Indra. A powerful, heroic god of weather and war in some Asian tales, akin to Zeus and Thor and other Indo-European deities.

Lotus: A flower that grows in ponds and lakes. The lotus has its roots in the muddy bottom, and its large and many-petaled flowers, floating on the water's surface, open to the light of the sun. The flower is a symbol of purity.

We are grateful for the opportunity to offer these Jataka tales to you. May they inspire fresh insight into the dynamics of human relationships and may understanding grow with each reading.

These adaptations of Jataka Tales are for children aged three to eight

JATAKA TALES SERIES